12 CHRISTMAS VOCAL SOLOS
FOR CLASSICAL SINGERS

To access companion recorded accompaniments online, visit:
www.halleonard.com/mylibrary

Enter Code
3387-3316-5177-3125

ISBN 978-1-4584-1378-9

G. SCHIRMER, *Inc.*

DISTRIBUTED BY
HAL•LEONARD®

Visit Hal Leonard Online at
www.halleonard.com

Contact us:
Hal Leonard
7777 West Bluemound Road
Milwaukee, WI 53213
Email: info@halleonard.com

In Europe, contact:
Hal Leonard Europe Limited
42 Wigmore Street
Marylebone, London, W1U 2RN
Email: info@halleonardeurope.com

In Australia, contact:
Hal Leonard Australia Pty. Ltd.
4 Lentara Court
Cheltenham, Victoria, 3192 Australia
Email: info@halleonard.com.au

CONTENTS

Pianist on the recordings:
Laura Ward

The price of this publication includes access to companion recorded accompaniments online,
for download or streaming, using the unique code found on the title page.
Visit **www.halleonard.com/mylibrary** and enter the access code.

GLORY HALLELUJAH TO DE NEW-BORN KING

(Christmas Spiritual)

African-American Spiritual
arranged by Hall Johnson

5

I call Je - sus de Won - der - ful Coun - sel - lor. Oh, _____

Glo - ry Hal - le - lu - jah! Oh, _____ Glo - ry Hal - le - lu - jah!

[*rit. last time*]

Fine

Glo - ry Hal - le - lu - jah to de new-born King. _ Jus' fol - low de Star _ an'

[*rit. last time*]

you'll find de Ba - by, Oh, _____ Glo - ry Hal - le - lu - jah! Oh, _____

Glory Hal-le-lu-jah! Glo-ry Hal-le-lu-jah to de new-born King._ You'll

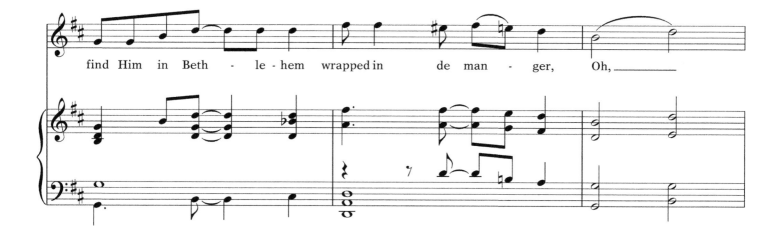

find Him in Beth - le-hem wrapped in de man - ger, Oh,_____

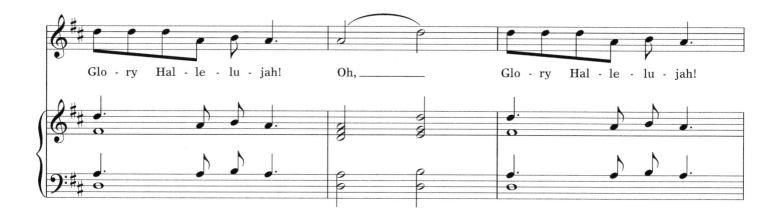

Glo-ry Hal - le - lu - jah! Oh,_____ Glo-ry Hal - le - lu - jah!

Glo-ry Hal - le -lu-jah to de new-born King._ Cry-in' "Peace on earth,_ good - will_

D.S. al Fine

I WONDER AS I WANDER
(Appalachian Carol)

Collected, adapted, and arranged by
John Jacob Niles

Espressivo ♩. = 60

I won-der as I wan-der, out un-der the sky, How Je-sus the Sav-ior did come for to die For poor on-'ry peo-ple like you and like I... I won-der as I wan-der, out un-der the sky.

When Ma - ry birthed Je - sus, 'twas in a cow's stall, With

wise men and farm - ers and shep-herds and all. But high from God's heav - en a

star's light did fall, And the prom - ise of a - ges it then did re - call.

If Je - sus had want - ed for an - y wee thing, A star in the sky, or a bird on the wing, Or all of God's an - gels in heav'n for to sing, He sure - ly could have it, 'cause he was the King.

I won - der as I wan - der, out un - der the sky, How

Je - sus the Sav - ior did come for to die For poor on - 'ry peo - ple like

you and like I... I won - der as I wan - der, out un - der the sky.

for Thomas Michael Tolliver Niles on being five years of age

JESUS, JESUS, REST YOUR HEAD

Adapted from the singing
of three people in Hardin County, Kentucky

Adapted by
John Jacob Niles

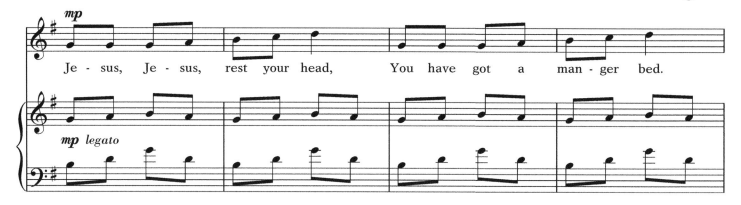

Je - sus, Je - sus, rest your head, You have got a man - ger bed.

All the mor - tal folk on earth Sleep in feath - ers at their birth.

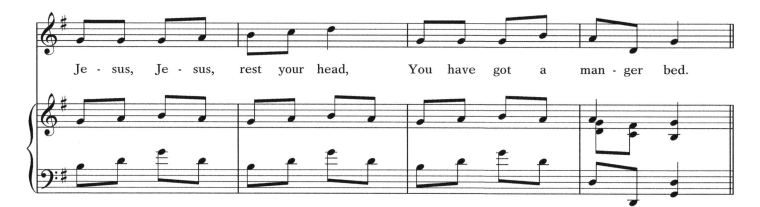

Je - sus, Je - sus, rest your head, You have got a man - ger bed.

All the mor-tal folk on earth Sleep in feath-ers at their birth.

Je-sus, Je-sus, rest your head, You have got a man-ger bed.

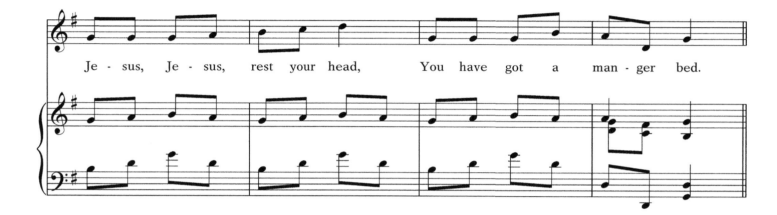

mf

2. To that man-ger came then wise men, Bring-ing things from hin and yon.

For the moth-er and the fa-ther And the bless-ed lit-tle Son.

Milk-maids left their fields and flocks And sat be-side the ass and ox.

Je-sus, Je-sus, rest your head, You have got a man-ger bed.

All the mor-tal folk on earth Sleep in feath-ers at their birth.

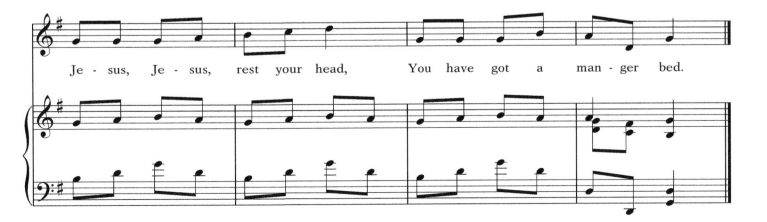

Je-sus, Je-sus, rest your head, You have got a man-ger bed.

LULLE LULLAY

Collected and arranged by
John Jacob Niles
adapted and arranged for voice and piano by
Bryan Stanley

With graceful movement

Lul - lay,_ Thou ti - ny lit - tle Child,_ Bye bye,_ lul - le,_ lul - lay;___ Lul - lay,_ Thou ti - ny lit - tle Child,_ Bye bye,_ lul - le,_ lul - lay.

Oh sis - ters two,＿ how may＿ we do＿ To per - se - vere＿ this

day?＿＿＿ To this＿ poor Young - ling for whom we sing＿ Bye - bye,＿ lul - le,＿ lul -

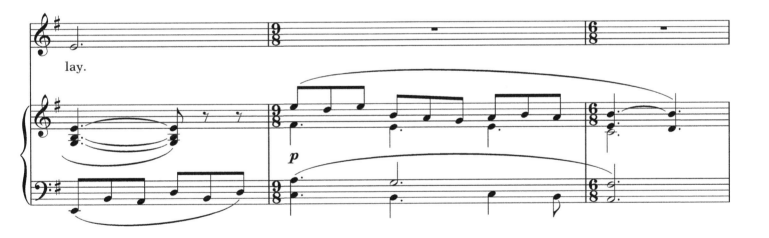

lay.

Her - od the King,＿＿ in ＿ his rag - ing, Charged＿ he hath this day＿＿ His

And when the stars in-gath - er do, In

their far ven - ture stay, Then smile as dream - ing,

Lit - tle One, Bye - bye, lul - le, lul - lay, bye -

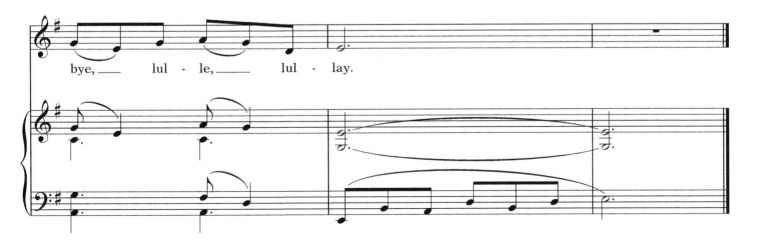

bye, lul - le, lul - lay.

MARY HAD A BABY
(Christmas Spiritual)

African-American Spiritual
arranged by Hall Johnson

Lullaby

*Johnson suggests singing the response "Yes, Lord" only in the verses beginning with the title.

MARY'S SOLILOQUY

from the cantata *The St. Luke Christmas Story*

Lucy Vessey

Cecil Effinger

Quietly (♩ = *c.* 84)

Mar-y heard the An-gels sing: "There shall be a lit-tle King

born to you, And He shall be___ Great-er than all roy-al-ty."

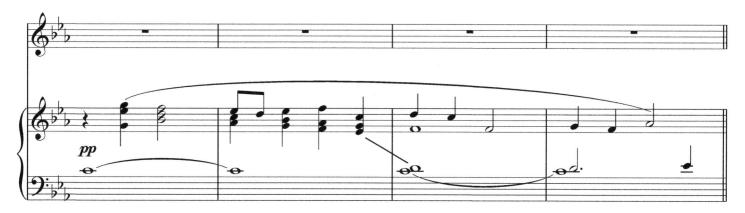

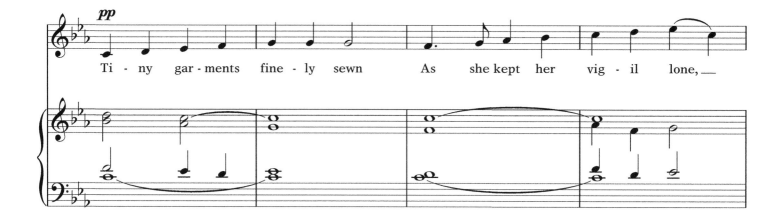

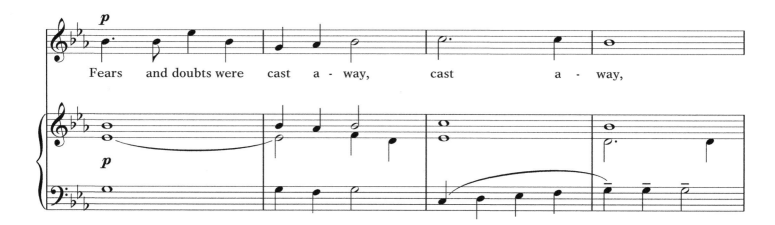

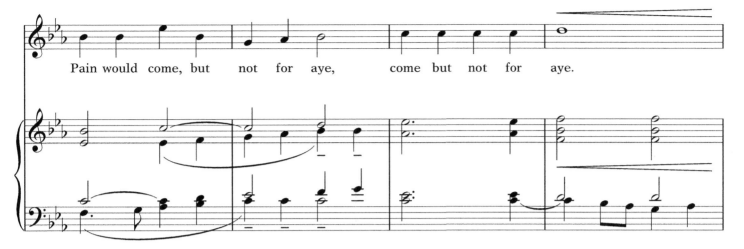

Pain would come, but not for aye, come but not for aye.

All would be for gain, not loss. Mar - y saw be - yond the cross,

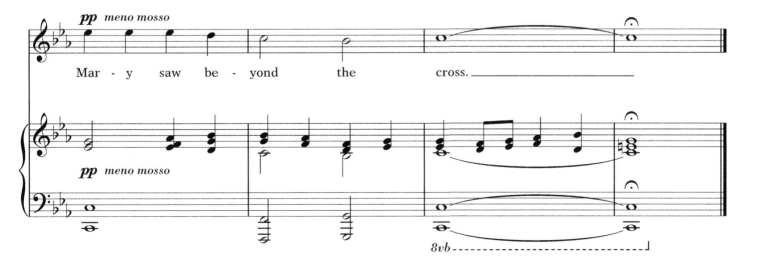

Mar - y saw be - yond the cross.

NOËL, NOËL, BELLS ARE RINGING

Alice Grainger★

Wilbur Chenoweth

★Words used by special permission.

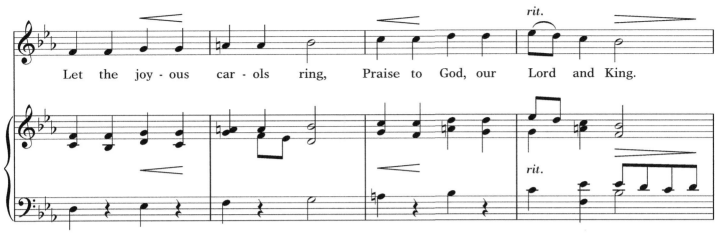

Let the joy-ous car-ols ring, Praise to God, our Lord and King.

No - ël, No - ël, Bells are ring - ing, Peace on earth this Christ - mas day.

No - ël, No - ël, Bells are ring - ing

through the clear and frost - y air. No - ël, No - ël, Glad - ness bring - ing

car - ols sweet from ev - 'ry - where. Once a - gain a star shines bright

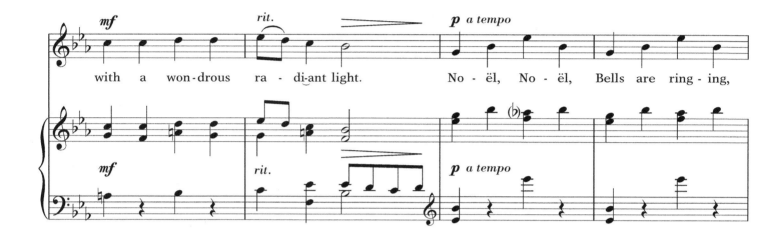

with a won - drous ra - di - ant light. No - ël, No - ël, Bells are ring - ing,

Peace on earth this Christ - mas day.

No - ël, No - ël, Bells are ring - ing, Peal - ing forth good - will and cheer.

No - ël, No - ël, Mu - sic wing - ing through the night in tones so clear.

May Thy love and peace a - bide on this hap - py Christ - mas tide.

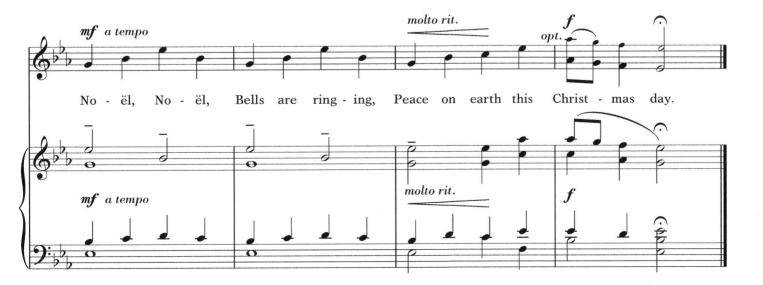

No - ël, No - ël, Bells are ring - ing, Peace on earth this Christ - mas day.

O HOLY NIGHT
(Cantique de Noël)

French Words by Placide Cappeau
English Words by John S. Dwight

Adolphe Adam

pin - ing, Till he ap - peared, and the soul felt its
nel - le Et de son père ar - rê - ter le cour-

worth. A thrill of hope the
roux. Le mon - de en - tier tres -

wea - ry world re - joic - es, For yon - der breaks a
sail - le d'es - pé - ran - ce A cet - te nuit qui

new and glo - rious morn. Fall on your
lui donne un sau - veur. Peu - ple, à ge -

knees! _____ Oh hear _____ the an - gel
noux! _____ at - tends _____ ta dé - li -

voic - es! O night _____ di -
vran - ce. No - ël! _____ No -

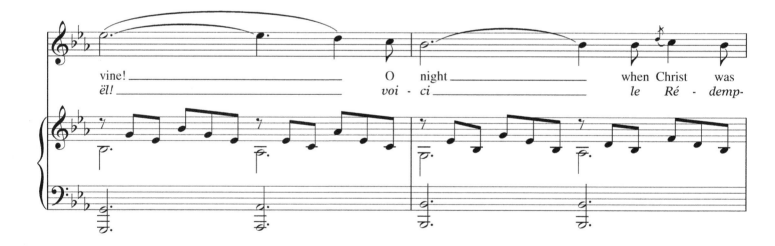

vine! _____ O night _____ when Christ was
ël! _____ voi - ci _____ le Ré - demp -

born, _____ O night _____ di -
teur, _____ No - ël! _____ No -

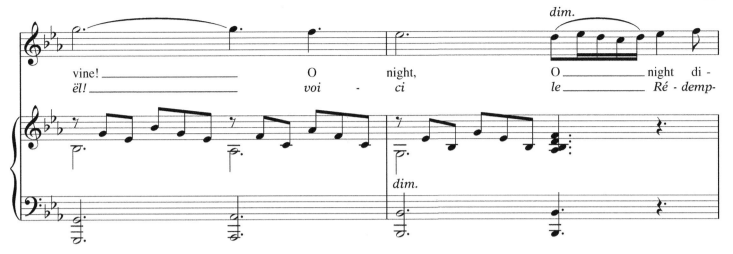

vine! _____ O night, O _____ night di -
ël! _____ voi - ci le _____ Ré - demp-

vine.
teur.

Tru - ly He taught us to love one an -
Le Ré - demp-teur a bri - sé tou - te en-

oth - er; His law is love and His Gos - pel is Peace.
tra - ve, La terre est li - bre et le ciel est ou - vert.

34

Chains shall He break, for the slave is our
Il voit un frè - re où n'é - tait qu'un es -

broth - er, And in His name____ all op - pres - sion shall
cla - ve, L'a-mour u - nit____ ceux qu'en-chaî - nait le

cease.   Sweet hymns of joy in
fer.   Qui lui di - ra no -

grate - ful cho - rus raise we, Let all with - in us
tre re - con - nais-san - ce? C'est pour nous tous qu'il

praise His Ho - ly name.___ Christ_____ is the
naît, qu'il souf - fre et meurt.___ Peu - ple, de -

Lord, then ev - er, ev - er
bout, chan - te ta dé - li -

praise we, His pow'r_____ and
vran - ce, No - ël!_____ No -

glo - ry___ ev - er - more pro -
ël!_____ chan - tons_____ le Ré - demp -

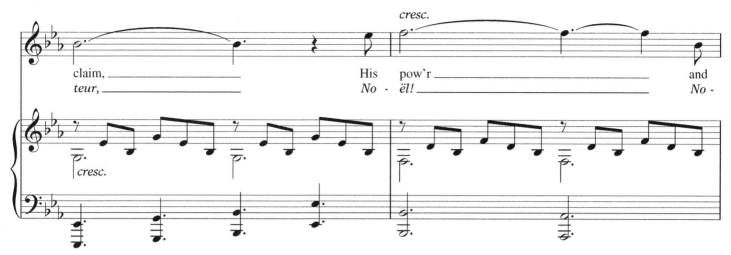

claim, _____ His pow'r _____ and
teur, _____ No - ël! _____ No -

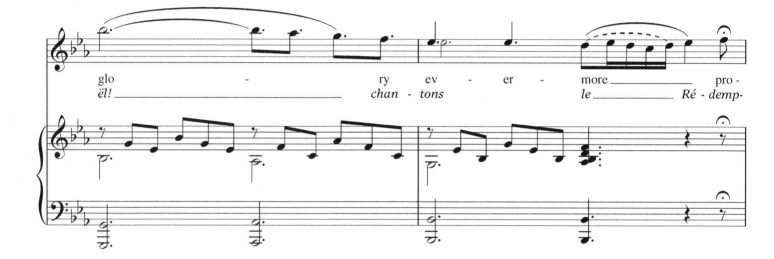

glo - ry ev - er - more _____ pro-
ël! _____ chan - tons le _____ Ré - demp-

claim.
teur.

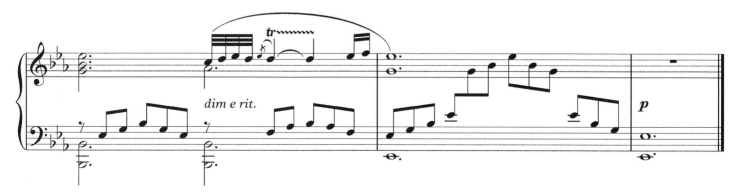

ON CHRISTMAS EVE

from *Five Christmas Songs*

Zacharias Topelius
English translation by Albert J. Hjerpe

Jean Sibelius
Op. 1, No. 3

SWEET LITTLE BOY JESUS

Words and Music by
John Jacob Niles

WHAT CHILD IS THIS?

William C. Dix

"Greensleeves"
Old English Melody
arranged by Ernst Victor Wolff

What Child is this,— who, laid to rest, On Ma - ry's lap— is sleep - ing? Whom an - gels greet— with an - thems sweet, While shep - herds watch are keep - ing?

This, this___ is Christ the King, Whom shep - herds guard_ and an - gels sing:

Haste, haste___ to bring Him laud, The Babe,___ the Son___ of

Ma - ry. Why lies He in___ such

mean es - tate___ Where ox and ass___ are feed - ing? Good

Christ - ian, fear: __ for sin - ners here The si - lent Word __ is plead - ing.

Nails, spear __ shall pierce Him through, The Cross be borne __ for me, for you:

Hail, hail __ the Word made flesh, __ The Babe, __ the Son __ of Ma - ry!

So bring Him in - cense, gold and myrrh, Come,

peas - ant, King __ to own Him, The King of kings __ sal - va - tion brings, Let

lov - ing hearts en - throne Him. Raise, raise __ the song on high; The

vir - gin sings __ her lull - a - by: Joy, joy, __ for Christ is born, The

Babe, __ the Son __ of Ma - ry!

WHAT SONGS WERE SUNG

Words and Music by
John Jacob Niles

stood hard by While heav'n-ly sound filled up the sky.

Now let us stand, un - cov-ered all, Be - fore this crèche in___

low - ly stall, Where kings and an - gels dig - ni - fy God's___ gift, His Son, in hu -

mil - i - ty. We do not know, we can-not tell What

46

songs were sung, what star-light fell, Or why the ho-ly mys-ter-y stands For

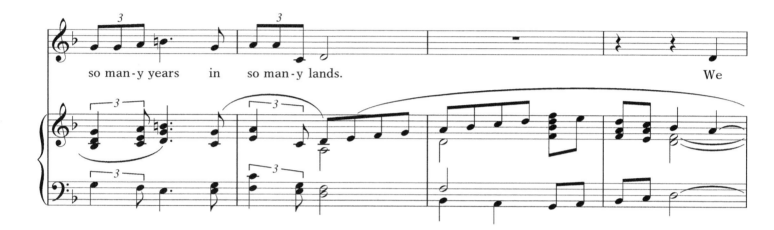

so man-y years in so man-y lands. We

can-not tell, we do not know What stars shone down so long a-go, When

Mar-y birthed her own sweet Son And peace and love be-came as one.